Speak His Words

IRA ROACH III

Copyright © 2014 Ira Roach III
All rights reserved. No part of this book shall be reproduced, stored in a retrieval system, or transmitted by any means without written permission from the publisher.

Unless noted, Scripture quotations are from THE HOLY BIBLE, NEW INTERNATIONAL VERSION®, NIV® Copyright © 1973, 1978, 1984, 2011 by Biblica, Inc.® Used by permission. All rights reserved worldwide.

ISBN: 9780615945767
Printed in the United States of America

Published by:
Speak Life Publishing, LLC
P.O. Box 1144
Baltimore, MD 21203
www.yelvaburley.com

DEDICATION

This first book is dedicated to the Dream Center members. You have stuck it out with me; you have prayed for me and you have encouraged me. People have often over-looked the talent, anointing, and strength of what lies beneath us because of the outer appearance. I'm truly glad that the God I serve doesn't look at our appearance but looks at our heart.

The Lord has bestowed upon me the fivefold office of Apostle and that could not have come to pass without your help. David led an army and yes he was the captain but it took the entire army to help him defeat those enemies that came up against the people of God.

"Speak His Words," is the weapon of choice to combat the enemy and his attack against God's people. We are not ignorant of Satan's devices and we will use the power of God's word to help us arrive to our next dimension in God.

CONTENTS

Acknowledgments

Introduction

	Subject	Page #
1	Abuse	2
2	Self-Addictions	4
3	Loved One Addictions	5
4	Backslidden	7
5	Baptism of the Holy Spirit	8
6	Death of a Loved One	10
7	Demonic Activity	11
8	Depression	13
9	Family Problems	15
10	Fear	17
11	Finances/Provision	19
12	Generational Curses	21
13	Healing	23
14	Job Problems	25
15	Seeking Employment	27
16	Marital Problems	29
17	Salvation for a Spouse	31
18	Wisdom & Guidance	33

ACKNOWLEDGMENTS

My father and bonus mother Ira and Carolyn Roach Jr. and my mother Margaret Neal who have been my motivation in life. Thank you for the prayers, private talks and seeing the example set before me.

My maternal grandmother Ruth V. Neal and Paternal grandmother Bertha E. Roach, thanks for the lessons of prayer, repentance and forgiveness, I miss you both more than anyone can imagine.

And last but not least, God my father who has allowed me to realize He has gifted me to reach the world through creativity.

ABUSE

Psalms 147:3
He heals the brokenhearted and binds up their wounds.

Isaiah 40:29-31
He gives power to the weak, and to those who have no might He increases strength…Those who wait on the LORD shall renew their strength; they shall mount up with wings like eagles, they shall run and not be weary, they shall walk and not faint.

Isaiah 54:14, 15
In righteousness you shall be established; you shall be far from oppression, for you shall not fear; and from terror, for it shall not come near you. Indeed they shall surely assemble, but not because of Me. Whoever assembles against you shall fall for your sake.

Isaiah 61:3
…To give them beauty for ashes, the oil of joy for mourning, the garment of praise for the spirit of heaviness…

PRAYER

Heavenly Father, thank you that Jesus came to heal the brokenhearted and bind their wounds. I ask you to give me strength and hope, beauty for ashes, and joy for mourning. Lord, I ask you to heal me from all past abuse and protect me from future abuse. Help me to forgive everyone who has hurt me in any way, in Jesus' name.

SELF ADDICTIONS

I John 1:9
If we confess our sins, He is faithful and just to forgive us our sins and to cleanse us from all unrighteousness.

John 8:36
Therefore if the Son makes you free, you shall be free indeed.

Romans 5:20
…But where sin abounded, grace abounded much more…

Romans 13:14
But put on the Lord Jesus Christ, and make no provision for the flesh, to fulfill its lusts.

PRAYER

Heavenly Father, I confess to you that I am in bondage to _____. Lord, I ask for your forgiveness and that you would cleanse me from all unrighteousness and renew a right spirit within me. I ask for greater strength to resist every temptation and to live righteously for you. I believe I receive that strength and freedom now, in the name of Jesus.

LOVED ONES ADDICTIONS

Jeremiah 32:27
Behold, I am the LORD, the God of all flesh. Is there anything too hard for Me?

I John 5:14-15
Now this is the confidence that we have in Him, that if we ask anything according to His will, He hears us. And if we know that He hears us, whatever we ask, we know that we have the petitions that we have asked of Him.

Philippians 4:6-7
Be anxious for nothing, but in everything by prayer and supplication, with thanksgiving, let your requests be made known to God; and the peace of God, which surpasses all understanding, will guard your hearts and minds through Christ Jesus.

I John 3:8-9
...For this purpose the Son of God was manifested, that He might destroy the works of the devil.

PRAYER

Heavenly Father, thank you that there is nothing too hard for you. Thank you that Jesus was manifested that He might destroy the works of the devil. Heavenly Father, I ask you to set _____ free from every bondage and addiction, in the name of Jesus. Lord, put a desire in their heart for righteousness. Thank you for answering my prayer, in Jesus' name.

BACKSLIDDEN

Jeremiah 3:22

...I will heal your backslidings.

John 14:15-16

If you love Me, keep My commandments.

Hebrews 8:12

For I will be merciful to their unrighteousness, and their sins and their lawless deeds I will remember no more.

I John 1:9

If we confess our sins, He is faithful and just to forgive us our sins and to cleanse us from all unrighteousness.

PRAYER

Heavenly Father, your Word says that if we confess our sins, you will forgive us and cleanse us from all unrighteousness. Lord, I ask you to cleanse _____ /or me from all sin in my life. Put right desires in my heart; restore my sensitivity to sin as You see it. Lord, help me/or to hunger and thirst after righteousness, in Jesus' name.

BAPTISM IN THE HOLY SPIRIT

John 7:38

He who believes in Me, as the Scripture has said, out of his heart will flow rivers of living water.

Luke 11:13

If you then, being evil, know how to give good gifts to your children, how much more will your heavenly Father give the Holy Spirit to those who ask Him!

Acts 2:4

And they were all filled with the Holy Spirit and began to speak with other tongues,
as the Spirit gave them utterance.

I Corinthians 14:4

He who speaks in a tongue edifies himself…

PRAYER

Heavenly Father, you promise to give the Holy Spirit to those who ask. You say we should be filled with the Spirit. Lord, I ask now that you would baptize me with your Holy Spirit with the evidence of speaking in tongues. I pray that rivers of living water would flow from me in the name of Jesus. I believe I receive this baptism—by faith—now, in Jesus' name. (Speaking in tongues is verbal, so you need to speak aloud. Start verbally praising the Lord in English. Then start yielding your tongue to whatever words form in your mouth. Keep doing this until you hear your Heavenly Language come forth. Do not get discouraged. Believe you have received and keep trying until it happens.)

DEATH OF A LOVED ONE

Matthew 5:4

Blessed are those who mourn, for they shall be comforted.

II Corinthians 1:3,4

Blessed be the God and Father of our Lord Jesus Christ, the Father of mercies and God of all comfort , who comforts us in all our tribulation, that we may be able to comfort those who are in any trouble, with the comfort with which we ourselves are comforted by God.

Psalms 147:3

He heals the brokenhearted and binds up their wounds.

PRAYER

Heavenly Father, thank you that you promise comfort to those who mourn. Heavenly Father, we know that you are the God of all comfort. Lord, we ask you to comfort and fill them with your peace. Give them the strength they need in this difficult time. We pray that you would surround them with your love. Heal their brokenness and bind their wounds, in Jesus name.

DEMONIC ACTIVITY

I John 3:8

...For this purpose the Son of God was manifested, that He might destroy the works of the devil.

Luke 10:19

...I give you the authority to trample on serpents and scorpions, and over all the power of the enemy, and nothing shall by any means hurt you.

II Corinthians 2:14

Now thanks be to God who always leads us in triumph in Christ...

John 8:36

Therefore if the Son makes you free, you shall be free indeed.

James 4:7

Therefore submit to God. Resist the devil and he will flee from you.

PRAYER

Heavenly Father, thank you that Jesus came to destroy the works of the devil. Thank you, Lord, that you always cause us to triumph and overcome. In the name of Jesus, I come against every work of the enemy and command the enemy to leave every situation in my life. I declare that I am free of every evil work by the blood of Jesus. Heavenly Father, I pray that your will and peace would be established in this situation, in Jesus' name.

DEPRESSION

Isaiah 61:3
…To give them beauty for ashes, the oil of joy for mourning, the garment of praise for the spirit of heaviness…

Psalms 145:14
The LORD upholds all who fall, and raises up all who are bowed down.

Psalms 34:18
The LORD is near to those who have a broken heart, and saves such as have a contrite spirit.

John 10:10
…I have come that they may have life, and that they may have it more abundantly.

PRAYER

Heavenly Father, you lift up those who are bowed down. Lord, I ask that you would lift me up and heal my brokenness. Give me beauty, joy, and praise instead of depression and heaviness. I resist depression, and I thank you for restoring my spirit and showing me how I can obtain that abundant life you have promised, in Jesus' name.

FAMILY PROBLEMS

Psalms 127:1

Unless the LORD builds the house, they labor in vain who build it; unless the LORD guards the city, the watchman stays awake in vain.

Isaiah 32:17-18

...And the effect of righteousness, quietness and assurance forever. My people will dwell in a peaceful habitation, in secure dwellings, and in quiet resting places...

Deuteronomy 26:11

So you shall rejoice in every good thing which the LORD your God has given to you and your house...

PRAYER

Heavenly Father, by faith we declare Jesus is Lord of this family and no weapon formed against them shall prosper. We come against all strife, discord, division, unforgiveness, anger or ill will, in the name of Jesus. We invite the power of the Holy Spirit to work in their lives. Thank you for establishing peace, harmony and unity into this family. Thank you for showing them how to love one another, as you have loved them, in Jesus' name.

FEAR

II Timothy 1:7

For God has not given us a spirit of fear, but of power and of love and of a sound mind.

Hebrews 13:6

…The LORD is my helper; I will not fear…

I John 4:18

There is no fear in love; but perfect love casts out fear, because fear involves torment.
But he who fears has not been made perfect in love.

John 14:27-28

Peace I leave with you, My peace I give to you; not as the world gives do I give to you.
Let not your heart be troubled, neither let it be afraid.

PRAYER

Heavenly Father, thank you that you have not given me a spirit of fear, but of love and power and a sound mind. Lord, I know that fear is not from you. You are the author of peace. I ask you to fill me with your peace. I resist all fear in the name of Jesus. Thank you that I have the peace of God that surpasses all understanding, in Jesus' name.

FINANCES / PROVISION

Matthew 7:7-9

Ask, and it will be given to you; seek, and you will find; knock, and it will be opened to you. For everyone who asks receives, and he who seeks finds, and to him who knocks it will be opened.

Hebrews 4:16

Let us therefore come boldly to the throne of grace, that we may obtain mercy and find grace to help in time of need.

Psalms 23:1

The LORD is my shepherd; I shall not want.

Luke 12:29-31

...Do not seek what you should eat or what you should drink, nor have an anxious mind... your Father knows that you need these things. But seek the kingdom of God, and all these things shall be added to you.

PRAYER

Heavenly Father, you say we can come boldly before you to ask for grace and mercy in time of need. You say that whoever asks, receives. Lord, I ask for grace and mercy and that you would meet this financial need, in the name of Jesus. Lord, I ask that you would teach me to prosper, help me to seek your kingdom and receive everything I need, in Jesus' name.

GENERATIONAL CURSES

Galatians 3:13

Christ has redeemed us from the curse of the law, having become a curse for us

(for it is written, "Cursed is everyone who hangs on a tree")…

John 10:10

The thief does not come except to steal, and to kill, and to destroy. I have come that

they may have life, and that they may have it more abundantly.

2 Corinthians 5:19

…God was in Christ reconciling the world to Himself, not imputing their trespasses to them…

Jeremiah 31:34

…For I will forgive their iniquity, and their sin I will remember no more.

PRAYER

Heavenly Father, thank you that Jesus has redeemed us from the curse. Thank you that you have forgiven my sins and do not count them against me. I accept your forgiveness and acknowledge that Jesus is the Lamb of God who takes away my sin and the sin of my family. I thank you that every generational curse is broken in my family, in the name of Jesus.

HEALING

Jeremiah 32:17

'Ah, Lord GOD! Behold, You have made the heavens and the earth by Your great power and outstretched arm. There is nothing too hard for You.

Isaiah 53:5

But He was wounded for our transgressions, He was bruised for our iniquities; The chastisement for our peace was upon Him, And by His stripes we are healed.

1 Peter 2:24-25

…Who Himself bore our sins in His own body on the tree, that we, having died to sins, might live for righteousness—by whose stripes you were healed.

Psalms 107:20

He sent His word and healed them, and delivered them from their destructions.

PRAYER

Heavenly Father, thank you that Jesus bore our grief, our sufferings and our sorrows, and that His wounds have healed ours. We know that nothing is too hard for you. Heavenly Father, we are praying and believing now for the complete healing and restoration of _____. Thank you Lord that you sent your Word and healed them, in Jesus' name.

JOB PROBLEMS

1 Corinthians 14:33

For God is not the author of confusion but of peace…

Psalms 55:22

Cast your burden on the LORD, And He shall sustain you; He shall never permit the righteous to be moved.

Psalms 55:18

He has redeemed my soul in peace from the battle that was against me…

Romans 8:28

And we know that all things work together for good to those who love God, to those who are the called according to His purpose.

PRAYER

Heavenly Father, your Word says you are not the author of confusion but of peace. You say we can cast our cares on you and you will sustain us. Lord, I cast this difficult work situation on you and ask that you would create peace and harmony in this matter. Thank you, Heavenly Father, for working all things together for my good, in Jesus' name.

SEEKING EMPLOYMENT

Mark 11:24

Therefore I say to you, whatever things you ask when you pray, believe that you
receive them, and you will have them.

Psalms 5:12

For You, O LORD, will bless the righteous; With favor You will surround him as with a shield.

James 1:5-6

If any of you lacks wisdom, let him ask of God, who gives to all liberally and without
reproach, and it will be given to him. But let him ask in faith, with no doubting...

Hebrews 11:1-2

Now faith is the substance of things hoped for, the evidence of things not seen.

PRAYER

Heavenly Father, your Word says that whatsoever things that we pray for if we believe we shall receive them, we will have them in the name of Jesus. Father, I ask you now to set aside a fulfilling job for me and one that will meet my financial needs. I thank you for directing me to the right place and giving me wisdom and favor. Even though I don't see this job now, by faith I am believing it will come, in Jesus' name.

MARITAL PROBLEMS

Jeremiah 32:27

Behold, I am the LORD, the God of all flesh. Is there anything too hard for Me?

Psalms 127:1

Unless the LORD builds the house, They labor in vain who build it; Unless the LORD guards the city, The watchman stays awake in vain.

Luke 1:37

For with God nothing will be impossible.

Isaiah 32:17-18

The work of righteousness will be peace, And the effect of righteousness, quietness and assurance forever. My people will dwell in a peaceful habitation, In secure dwellings, and in quiet resting places…

PRAYER

Heavenly Father, we thank you that you there is nothing too hard for you, and all things are possible to those who believe. In the name of Jesus, we are praying and believing for reconciliation and peace in the marriage of _____. We thank you, Lord, for establishing peace, harmony, and unity in this marriage. We declare _____ and _____ are of one mind, one accord, and one flesh. We ask that you would bless this marriage and show them how to love one another, in Jesus' name.

SALVATION FOR A SPOUSE

Mark 11:24

Therefore I say to you, whatever things you ask when you pray, believe that you
receive them, and you will have them.

2 Peter 3:9

The Lord is not slack concerning His promise, as some count slackness, but is longsuffering toward us, not willing that any should perish but that all should come to repentance.

Galatians 5:6

For in Christ Jesus neither circumcision nor uncircumcision avails anything, but faith working through love.

PRAYER

Heavenly Father, you say whatsoever things that we pray for, if we believe we receive, we shall have it, in the name of Jesus. Heavenly Father, We know it is Your desire is for all men to be saved and come to a knowledge of the truth. Lord, I am believing now for the salvation of my spouse. I ask that you bring them to knowledge of the truth. Lord, show me how to love them as I wait. I pray this in Jesus' name.

WISDOM AND GUIDANCE

James 1:5-6
If any of you lacks wisdom, let him ask of God, who gives to all liberally and
without reproach, and it will be given to him.

John 10:27
My sheep hear My voice, and I know them, and they follow Me.

Psalms 37:23
The steps of a good man are ordered by the LORD...

Psalms 32:8
I will instruct you and teach you in the way you should go; I will guide you with My eye.

PRAYER

Lord, you say if we lack knowledge, we can ask and you will give it to us freely. I ask for your wisdom and guidance in my life. I ask that you would reveal your will to me and help me to hear your voice in all things. Thank you for ordering my steps and making them sure, in Jesus' name.

ABOUT THE AUTHOR

Apostle Ira D. Roach III a native of Georgetown, DE was born April 20, 1971 to Ira D. Roach Jr.(Carolyn Y. Roach) and Margaret Neal. He is a Senior Pastor, Life Coach, Entrepreneur, Mentor, Motivational Speaker, Guardian, and Writer. He has overcome many obstacles to arrive at this place in his life. Apostle Roach was reared in the gospel at 7th Day Holy Church of Deliverance under the tutelage of Bishop Mary L. Alexander and Elder Austin Alexander since the year 1992. He has served in various capacities including; Praise and Worship Leader, Choir Member, Deacon, Minister, Elder, and Youth Pastor. His sole desire is to help people discover their hidden talents and live life to the fullest. In the year 2004 he was commissioned by the Lord to found the City of Refuge Inc under the covering of Apostle Ivory Jenkins and Apostle Jenkins consecrated him as a Bishop in 2007. May, 2009 he acknowledged the Five-Fold ministry on his life and received the Apostolic Succession from Apostle Anthony G. Armstrong.

He has a testimony of being "impoverished" in his thinking for many years but has realized that it is the Lord that gives us the power to get wealth. Ira is a gifted speaker, inspiring preacher and insightful spiritual director who presents the answers to life's questions in an easy to understand way. He speaks from his many experiences from his bouts with low self-esteem, depression and anger issues. Mr. Roach has served communities in the rural areas and small towns of Delaware, lower Maryland, the Jersey shore and most recently Baltimore. His inspirational talks and presentations always contain his sincerity of faith, genuine spirit, enthusiasm and comical frankness that have changed hearts, minds and the lives of many. Young, old, and middle aged is his focus audience, but he especially has a genuine love for helping at-risk young people. His message remains the same, "you can do all things through Christ that strengthens you."

(Continued on the next page)

He formed Idrch3 Ministries in 2009, but has been doing the work of a non-profit agency for a number of years. His hope is to reach a larger audience through a 501(c) (3) organization by enhancing the services already being offered. To date Idrch3 Ministries is responsible for BER Christian Academy (a program for high school drop outs to receive a diploma with a graduation in Cap & Gown), The Leadership Institute (programs for biblical teaching and ministry focus), Duro Entertainment (a theater group producing plays for the entire family). Ira holds numerous degrees which include; Associates in Early Childhood Education, Bachelors of Arts in Counseling, and a Doctorate of Christian Education which he earned in 2006. Currently he is pursuing his PH.D in Christian Counseling. He is a father, preacher, teacher, prophet, and slave to the Gospel.

www.ingramcontent.com/pod-product-compliance
Lightning Source LLC
Chambersburg PA
CBHW070751050426
42449CB00010B/2427